Look Up

Poems for a Life

Maureen Geraghty

ISBN:0615859321
ISBN-13:9780615859323

DEDICATION

For Henry and Lucy,
my fiercest loves

CONTENTS

Advice I Wish I'd Been Given

Your life will not be neat.
Not what you plotted, perhaps even wanted.
I attempt not to mow fields of daisies, nor storm
a sunny picnic. These words are here simply to
soothe unsettled, sleepless nights of doubt,
the "where-did-I-go-wrong" reaper whose
thievery is to convince dream's death.

You have not failed.
The moon is still full, will yet spill its milky
Orb when darkness seems
the only thing on your path.
When not a single thing sings
and what comes was never your wish—
Burn the map you've clung to, rest by its warmth
while life's story spins you out
of succulent, silent cocoon.
If doves disappear in the tree,
and ocean gleams meek,
if head bows under thunderous thoughts—

Don't seek sense.
Unpeel what veils the juice of fruit.
Open toward uninvited visitors.
See what's before you.
Listen.

Go

The oldest cave God made
          is in your Heart.
                    Go there.
Sit in its murky solitude.
                    Be silent.
Where it's broken,
                    spears of light linger................

In Your Life

There might be three people
Three, if you are extremely lucky
A trinity of those
who will walk your path--
Three who hold no judgment within their callused
offering hands.

There could be two,
Possibly three that stick around
through both Grit and Glory
Two or three who don't
ask a penny for your thoughts
But, instead, lend listening ears for free.

Pray for One, hopefully two or three
You can trust like honest blood,
companions courageous enough--
raw & confident-sufficient.
Willing to risk it all--
cup Glitter and Grime
in their own bruised palms
focused on miracles
disinterested in your pile of sin.

Feel blessed with two, or three or one
that you call Friend--
That you know as Real
whose weather is not fair
but rather, blazes as Super Nova
steady through a life-long sky:
dark, dark nights, sublime suns.

Those who refuse to fall as passing stars bargaining
promise or wish.
Know that two, occasionally one or three
will look long enough to see--
See you through it all.

Revolt

Daily descriptions of violence, injury,
love gone wrong
stain the pages of history--
Crack & shatter under grueling weight.
World becomes intolerant of heavy, horrifying, of
Un-tempered hate.
Weary of pain & distress,
So from now on...
Burden will birth beauty,
Grotesque plans for Grand.
Constellations vow transformation:

Sickness & grief push brittle wings through cocoons,
fly to a better place.
Stories of greed & abduction,
brutality & terror
weave themselves an afghan at your feet.

Accounts of cancer, fraud, & child porn
blend butter & sugar into fresh-baked pastries.
Reports of poverty, deception and rotten meat
spin soil into earthen pots
from which children sip spring water.
Beatings, bigotry and global warming
Paint blue wooden sailboats
breeze 'cross placid sea
toward orange-ribbon horizons.
Cholera, cocaine and sabotage
translate to notes of a harp.
Gossip, libel, profanity
speak themselves a sweet verse,
spill on lonely ears,
whisper tender secret.

Graffiti, gang signs, and smog
combine elements, create crimson ember for
campfire marshmallows.
Drones, guns, & A-bombs seek repentance
through silk, yarn, and beach glass.

The Cosmos decided we've been bitter too long.
Universe, bored of Oppression—
restores in
Revolt.

Boston

The Buddhist says it's a good sign
that we feel outrage, grief--
mourn atrocities.
It means hurting humans
still shocks our still sensitive soul.
We've managed, collectively, not to
become jaded & numb
after centuries—incident after incident
of blood, bomb, & dead child,
the wailing of ones left with loss.
We've kept shiny, that jewel deep down
which continues to cry for the stranger
that knows pain is thinner, shared.

Blessings

(inspired by John O'Donahue)

On the days where the sun's butter cannot
warm your marrow chill
The times when you wear the gray blanket of despair
Your lids too weighty to allow entrance of light
For moments when the arrow
has struck too close to vein.
When the body is carried like a
shadowy suitcase of leaden bones.

At those points in time when time points back its
sharpened blade
And the air is stale
--it's all you can do to swallow next billowed breath
On days where the angels have taken to their caves
and Hope is a distant island in a craggy pond
When the birds seem to have lost
choreographed pattern and instead
shatter the sky in black stain
When loneliness wraps you in a bitter wind....

May ribbons of orange and yellow sunrise
draw you out the open door
Let velvet, fine silk adorn
the landscape of your skin.
Invite the candle housed within your ribs
to burn white light guiding you
where you know
as Home.

Accept offerings of outstretched arms
of open palms,
one hand to hold.
May your eyes drink
from a vase of fresh lilacs,
sip ocean's foamy crescent.
May the violin's bow glide through you
a rhythm, a dance
a stroke of peace.
Let threads of green grass
weave a path toward new wilderness--
a grand palace of wild
where you breathe clover-scented air.
On a bed of moss, lay down your flamed body
and rest.

Solitude

Does anyone understand
the foam marrow need
Of Solitude?
I'm not talking, "Wouldn't it be nice
to have time alone."

I mean oxygen & blood.

Forty-Eight
(modeled after "Eleven" by Sandra Cisneros)

What they don't tell you is that when
you're forty-eight, you are also thirty-two and
twenty-six, eighteen, twelve and six and one.
You wake up, all forty-eight years stacked in the bed
but when you close your eyes, you feel twenty six,
invincible.
Like when you stayed up talking on the phone way
past midnight and still had to get up at five. In your
twenties, you could pull it off, but forty-eight
drags through the next day, baggy-eyed & crabby.

Or some days you hear yourself arguing with your
six-year-old telling her to act her age, and that's
exactly what she's doing but you're stuck in twelve
when you tried to act grown but inside felt like a
crumbly kid.

Some days you just want adults to do the work while
you read magazines, sit on a beach. Like at fifteen
when you knew everything, had your life graphed in
storybook timelines, when bad things wouldn't
happen because you pushed at perfection until it
hurt.

What they don't understand is that at forty-eight,
you still cuss, still say things so mean & bargain with
God that you'll be soooo good if this One Time, those
words were scratched from the record, deleted.

Some days forty-eight acts like three,
hiding behind Mom's leg when students, kids, lovers
expect answers & you have no choice
but to whimper, "I don't know."
Sometimes you want to cry all day, but need to wear
your forty-eight face like you're all glued together,
all fixed & fine.

Some days, you are sixteen and it is all about
you. Everything is personal
and you just want someone to deliver a helium
balloon bouquet, a dozen roses,
have the world confirm you are special.

Today I wish I was one hundred and two, taking slow
walks after tea in the morning, writing at a wooden
desk at noon, sitting on my porch at dusk—rocking,
singing, laughing not thinking one moment about
numbers, about time, about what was or will be.

Raise

Raise the roof
Raise your hand
Raise your glass
Raise Cain
Raise money
Raise the dead
Raise hell
Raise puppies
Raise your grades
Raise my eyebrow
Raise awareness
Raise my voice

Raise children

Behold

I pick up her one-year-old body
Writhing, squirming to break free.
The chubby branch of her arm held out,
palm upward
As if to say," Behold".

She is reaching for anything.
Desperate to make contact,
to study life with her fingers.
I hand her a Q-tip, a bank receipt, a rock
All of equal value while she scours
the world in awe.

It all makes sense now.
This innate desire
to gather, to marvel
simply wanting something to hold.

For Lucy who Woke up Sobbing

Your budding body just needs to cry.
All your two feet assertions about how
you can do it by yourself,
how you are a big girl.
Now, a tired space that just wants to be two years old.
To be held,
to cry into the cavernous shelter of your mommy's
chest.
You surrender the laborious effort to grow up
just enough for Momma to stroke
your tear-soaked hair.

Lingering in your relenting moments,
how your skin smells of talcum & cinnamon--
Cry, little one, cry.
You baptize us both.

DisOrder

Whoever thought it a good idea to give
young children puzzles?
Disney themes, barnyard scenes, the pile of kittens.
So many damn pieces
Scattered and stuffed
Mostly ignored, my daughter gnaws their edges until
the parts are soggy biscuits
I just keep picking up
embodying Sisyphus
plodding along daily, hourly, returning
trinkets to bin or basket.
Along comes the three foot Tasmanian devil, dumping
and throwing, kicking up dust-
then me, knuckles dragging on the floor, once again
tidying up, arranging-
dervishly whirling through his bedroom.

I am ziplocking, color coding, duct taping.
I just want one clean counter,
a room I don't have to kick my way into.
My thoughts reflect a hazy mirror of
dinosaur stickers, unjacketed library books,
half a Barbie, a Crayola tagged wall.
Frantic with the clutter of jovially named diesel engines,
I wish to design toys with the neurotic parent in mind.
Toys with an automatic sanitizer.
Games that avoid repetitive jingles-"stir, stir, stir the
soup" haunts my head.
The nightmares of Old MacDonald and his farm
while everyone is asleep and things are finally quiet.
Finally.
I'd choose Ravi Shankar or Gregorian Chants
to meditatively hum through plethora of plastic.

My toys would be pretty;
soft velvets, suede, and earth tones-
no neon too bright for caffeine dilated eyes.
And puzzles with three pieces-- tops. Three big pieces .
Family friendly toys.
Perhaps an Easybake Oven which converts to a bar
where Dora the Explorer mixes mojitos at happy hour
and The Wiggles croon Death Cab for Cutie tunes.
I try these ideas out on my son
who looks with raised eyebrow as if I told
him broccoli now comes chocolate flavored.
"That's silly." And he's off crashing
a dump truck into the dog.

Deep Country

This land is familiar--
its fragility of ground
lungs choke solely in exhale--
spit of acid rain.
One must travel this barren
to exit shallow.
Wait for the Deep Country.
Open hearted, it will find you.

Morning Lyric

Every morning
regardless of what midnight mailed,
your two globes open
woken by a sea of sun.
The finches fly to suet feeder
outside a breakfast window
where you admire the architecture of wings,
ponder levity and quest for sky.
Sky--- crevasse between mounds of cumulous,
blue cream frosting of unknown.

Perhaps you've given up on flight,
on atmospheric adventure.
Perhaps one leaden foot in front
of the other is endeavor plenty.
Yet, every morning
with open-mouthed glory
exists fresh chance to hear
the unfinished lyrics of your life,
the song you may hum into being.

Maybe not morning at all
but during gospel of dusk
when the owl begins her passage of Hope,
silent through din of nights
until an unexpected flash of finches
rouse anew.

Forest Run

There is something primal
about feet hitting trail- methodically, meditatively.
Red earth under soles
stitching seams through cathedral of Chinese Cork,
Basket Oak, Sequoia--
Body thumps earthy path
losing my way in wild: bark, moss, root.
Branches spread fingers baubled with emerald gems,
shimmering sunlight.
Bounding directionless through a curtain of leaves
running forward back into myself--
O Feral Me.

Love Arrives

Just when you thought it too late--
the dinner plate quietly set for one
dreams of companionship tucked in the attic
under piles of dusty letters and creaky memories
Love arrives--
slippery and unexpected, shaking this solitude

Just when you thought it too late
that Love forgot your address, skipped your name on
the love roster
when your bruised heart had, at last, resigned the
fruitless search.

Just when you thought it too late
Love crept in wearing slippers,
slid in through the cracks.
Initially, whispering secret songs
later, unmistakably announcing itself
like cayenne pepper on the tongue-
busting cobwebs, digging roots

Just when you thought it too late-
earth dry and the branches bare
Love woke winters,
launched colorful balloons, lit votives and
changed pronouns
Just then --
Love brashly tapped a shoulder
reminding of its solace, its celebration.
it's never too late.

Sugar

The waitress asks if I'd like coffee.
I nod, watch her set down steaming mug.
She clinks brew beside
ceramic bowl of sugar cubes.
As I lean into first sip of morning,
eyes fixate on geometry of sweet.
Perfect squares--
granules held together by refracting light.
Blocks of bliss
wait patiently in a dish--
magic melt on lips,
gritty & glorious --
Prayer for a mouth.

I think of you.

Rock, Rain, Real

I've read a thousand love poems-
tried to use one,
offer words of another passion-drunk
to You, keeper of my life juice.
None will do--
Like pretty petals breathed by a spring wind,
their loveliness holds no weight,
unable to anchor our ocean.
Shiny metaphors,
pearly rhymes & lacquered stanzas
wilt the altitude We climb.
Words I attempt to gather, arrange--
bones lacking meat of buttered fire.
Meandyou
are rock, rain, real.

This warm shadow,
this everynightgooddream,
blunt bliss, lush kiss---
I can't find that poem
so I write to inform
how YouandMe
encourage doubt of war
provide strength at surrender
electrify- skin to bone
send soul straight to temple.

Volumes of poetry I've scoured
explode a dusky sky--
turn Milky Way inside out.
Comets' expanse echo energy of lips on lips
yet pale single chest-chamber beat.

Silence & blank page more justly
represent four letters swimming my spirit.
grander, rounder & riper than past poet's ink.

I offer no words
silkier than YouandMe--
rock, rain, real.

Despite

We labor in gardens
Poke fingers in dirt
Fill holes with seeds
Weed and water
Groom rows of beans, marigolds
Every night scrub dirt from fingernails
Yet, despite such tenderness
plants die before reaching earth's surface.
Then,
There are those self–starters--
One breeze is all it takes
to guide seed to soil-- effortless meandering meadow.
Oak trunk pushes through crack of cement.

Campers rub together the driest sticks
Feed pine needles, kindling to hot orange embers
Still, fire does not stir.
But a blaze that leaves its charred claws
on miles of forest began as flick of cigarette ash.

There are truths we don't want to believe—
Control we wear like a tight suit
as if schedule and desire
guarantee Universal obedience
Work and will; pale charade
against spinning script of Cosmos.

Before You Go

Before you go, sit on a bench in the park,
Inhale seam between day & dusk.
Before you go, learn a neighbor's name,
make soup you will then share. At least,
make time for a handwritten letter
whether you send or not—
your hand, your thoughts on paper will help.

Before you go, tell one secret
for it may be a thread to a mystery you need to know.
Before you go, skip work for a nap,
Perhaps hop on a bike without map or plan.
Feel the sharp & attentive wind graze your face
exalting dandelions, lamenting no thing.
Go to the cinema alone, be the one laughing.

Look Up

The days stitch together our hundred thoughts.
A life, necklace of strung moments--
broken baubles, some low carat diamonds.
Today, sparkle-
a flash of syllable & sentiment.
This morning, an extra chance.
Geese arrow a grand redemption
as if to call out, "Look,
Look, there is still wide ceiling of sky!"
Frosted palette offering
blank-ness, silent whale of air-ocean.
Look up. The canopy writes in cirrus-ink.
Wispy smoke signals sing, " This is your life.
Open, open again."
The geese stain flight pattern toward somewhere,
keep pointing forward and forward.
Look up. The sun.
This moment is ours.

Wish To Be Broke

The Sufi mystic warns
against accepting the counterfeit coin
of momentary pleasure--
Throw all your pennies into the fountain. Wish
to be broke. Cheap imposters rob a heart.
Release the thief & instead
follow waters that flow downward
humbly quenching parched parts--
Ice into steam
beading air with intangible passions
neither trapped nor tamed—
constant as Sufi's sage syllables,
"Maybe the one I love is everywhere."

Life is a Metaphor

Memories are a son of a bitch
Our conversation, now a stain
The bed, a cage of wild animals
Blankets ooze cherries
His wrist is my mitten
My prayer is a shirt
Today, I am a splendid solar system.

Negative Simile Them

Their embrace was *not* as if
something real was being held
But more like the metal arm that grabs random prize
from vending machine-- act of duty
hardly worth a quarter.
The way they spoke was *not* like people who cared
about words going back & forth
from each other's shore,
but as if sounds were smog puffing
out the chimney of their mouths.
The Love they once ate from, *no longer*
a dripping peach.

If I was a Poem

What would I say?
Something quiet and true
Words that paint fresh, the sallow & blue
I'd capture silence, the wished for,
aches and the pain
I'd spell it on paper 'til peace came again
Syllables, consonants, refrain & rhymes
Salve and kindness for difficult times

Jokes, puns & random stabs at wit
Literary shade tree under which one could sit
I'd wish to connect readers' head to their heart
Build bridges in soul holes
Pages to ponder, space to start

A poem shakes dust toward sparkling new planet
Four dimensions rock haiku, limerick or sonnet
The meek find a voice, one profound song
Single sun-filled day where nothing went wrong

Although thoughts hold no magic for universal change
Pulsating wonder a poem can arrange.

Where Were You

when the stars bit the black blanket
into chunks of icy light?
When roots, stems, gritty soil slapped
palms with the sun 'til tomatoes dripped
inside their veiny skins?
Where were you when the bruises were blue,
when water fell for six days,
when I chipped my heart
and all the wind chimes plinked your name?

A Visit Home

We sit at the kitchen table.
Sip strong coffee.
He brings mug to mouth,
his hand—a map of dark veins--
starts sentences like,
"When I am gone" or
"After I die"
My jaw clenches & part of me leaves my body
anywhere, anything than
past-tense Father.

Logistics dispersed like pennies from a pocket:
accounts, documents, plots;
words like 'estate', 'executor', 'visitation mass'
I both savor this man I am from
& shiver thoughts of his gone.

This talk is not about me--
my discomfort, tears or torment.
My father requires a voice,
needs to speak to his eighty three years
needs to lie down tonight reading a mystery novel
content, having given thumbs-up to Non-Life--
winked acceptance
so when last breath is breathed,
he is free--
liberated to leave his children
safe, unfettered
on other side of Life's gauzy curtain.

Some Questions for The Virgin

I want to know more about you, Mary,
Mother of God. Mother of Jesus.
You are adored for your virginal conception
But how did you experience motherhood?
How were you were able to encourage, support and
create
a son who'd vow to save the world?
Was it inspirational bedtime stories?
Special summer camps?
How did you teach him to share, and so well?
O Mother of God, what would you
tell us of Jesus' tantrums?
The exhausting nights you mopped his feverish brow
while your bones ached with love for him.
Were you, at times, frustrated and bored?
Did you always keep your cool?
Or were there times that you wanted to cancel the
contract feeling completely unqualified
for the job of raising The Divine?
Did you have aspirations of your own?
Hobbies? Talents?
I have to believe your witty and determined self
sculpted space for a babe, would-be savior.
You were a damn good mom.
And as the flower is admired despite the work of the
dirt and sun,
Jesus gets the credit.
Yet, he was the sweet fruit of your generosity, sacrifice,
and playfulness.
Mary, what if you had *more* kids? Multiple messiahs.
Consider the possibilities.
Or, if you had none. If you burned your own candle
and lit up the skies with O Holy You.
Your maternal benevolence may have been just what

Earth needed to be peaceful, to be sane.
But, perhaps a child was essential.
Possibly, Jesus was your muse, your vessel of potential.
Mary, maybe—like many of us,
even *you* required a child
as a second chance to love yourself.
And then to have to let him go.
To give him up for the world.
Were you tempted to pack a bag and run, Jesus and
you, to somewhere warm and simple?
Escape to a beach in Mexico where you could just play
games and sing silly songs.
Eventually enroll him in preschool?
Shelter him from all the redeemer hubbub,
Keep him safe and happy and brimming with love?

What does it take, Mary, to make a Jesus?

Holy Whole

Forget Pearly Gates
Cherubs on Puffy Clouds

Look out the window.
Better yet, walk into
the hills that steeple into rolling churches.
Kneel at that alter—
Rock & red dirt.

Listen to the dimpled earth
sing through pine, moss & stream.

See grain and grass velvet the land
longer than forever.

Haily

Love, a Third World
for the girl who puts her Jack-Danieled mom to bed, the
girl whose body, violated while others played
Barbies or baseball.

Love, a stain
on the scabbed scars of girl who moved
with Grandma after Dad pointed pistol at Mom until
whining sirens scurried him away, forever a blur.

Love, a revolving door
of step-dads, bar-bought-boyfriends
new dude to whom Mom defers, defends
men who make good, filthy.

Love, the numb-
girl disappears through a hit,
a line, a couple pills.

Love, a way out-
hell bent to heal.
Run, girl
run into what Shines.

How We Live

For granted taking
Finger shaking
In our boots quaking
Truth forsaking
Through the coals raking
Heart breaking
Intoxicant partaking
Scared but faking
All in attempts at
Meaning making...

Connected

is the blue horizon to the brown earth
webs into mysterious orbits, comets, showers of meteor
fall to the ground in some meadow of Queen Anne's
Lace & daisies wrap round in a chain—
crown of a little girl
whose body once grew, bone by bone by eye by toe
inside body of her mother
who connects us all somehow, our mothers
through gush of love or gouge & scars
we share on skin & heart, seams that mend
us back to our selves
all begin naked and end in ash
gray confetti thrown from our fire
sitting cross legged together, mesmerized & warm
after the long day, connected by night and longing
and curtains of dream.

Dead

We are cuddled on the couch reading a story.
You look up to ask,
"When the fish eats the worm,
will the worm be dead?"
Earlier, nose pressed to the screen door,
 "Mommy, that fly is dead."
We walk across a parking lot,
"Are we holding hands so I won't get dead?"
Dead.
You, at three and a half, now grapple with
the existential.
How do I begin to describe this fragile flash
between alive and not?

As you practice this new vocabulary,
I sense your organic pureness tainted.
I puff the air out of my cheeks--
impending thoughts of future
subjects I'd rather avoid.

I stare into your full moon eyes ready to admit prickly
truths--
No, the old cat did not go to the farm.
The lion on Animal Planet *will* kill the gazelle.
However I sugar it—passing, heaven, cycle of life,
even a mother cannot pretty death.

"Yes, my love, the worm will die."
You nod, snuggle warm into my ribs,
 and gaze at the page as if death
was as natural as it is supposed to be.

Owies

You are fascinated with wounds-
Cuts, bumps and scrapes;
little jewels you adorn.
Bruises collected like Boy Scout badges
Every scar, a story
Slowly marring your pre-school porcelain
Making maps of accidents and abrasions.
You are awed by blood--
how it comes from inside your body, out.
How injury can produce deep red ooze.
You beg for Band Aids--
I peel off the white papers,
Lay the strip carefully to cover what is painful--
something you'll do forever.
You look up at me with watery eyes and sigh
truly believing my loving acts will make hurt disappear.

I want to Tylenol you into adolescence, into adulthood
Provide preventative elixir for six stitches to your chin
for black eyes and broken femurs
Make a Band-Aid bubble to cushion your tender being
from playground bullies, from being last picked for the
kickball team
from future tyrants and girls who will trample your
heart.

For now, I kiss each owie,
promise to make it better,
reach for the tin box of sticky gauze patches
and convince myself
love *will* make pain go away.

Resurrect Her in Chocolate

Bunnies and jelly beans-- easier language
than nails through bloody palms.
But the six-year-old wants more than sugar.
She hunts meaning--
Bigger treats: Rejuvenation, Reconciliation.
Her thirty-five pounds of weighty questions--
War, Divorce, Angels
Between platter of glazed ham & Yukon Golds
connects dots between
Reese's Pieces & Mary Magdalene
I drop metaphors: dark winter spins
toward tulips, night eventually opens day.
She smiles, wise Buddha-like
filled with chocolate & possibility.

Camera Fish

While the other children jerk metal handled nets from
a shallow lake, cast lines laced with earthworms,
cheer one another's catch: A Blue Gill, Sunfish, Crappie
sparkle-finned, writhing on hook & mesh—
My son walks away.
He looked into the fish's one eye as it hung, tail flailing
noticed its pierced jaw,
the way it danced desperation.
"I feel sorry for the fish", slumping away from pier.
I hand him my camera.
While the others continue to bait & lure
He snaps pictures,
captures the sun diamonding across water,
a melon colored Tiger Lily,
silhouette of kids lined up,
leaning in concentration.
His focus on Life-- too, too sensitive
for fate of a fish.

Two Wheeler

I give her a little push from the back
Pedal, pedal, pedal
She glides the parking lot
on two wheels
grinning through wide turns
glittery pink tassels on handlebars waving her glory.

It's about balance,
attention.

She gives it some gas with her brawny, scuffed legs
Pump, pump, pump
Gripping and braking
graceful figure eights
No more training for this girl.

It's about confidence, autonomy.

She saddles her banana seat,
holds handlebars as if reigning in a quarter horse.
Two wheels, one girl, twelve scrapes.
She concentrates on bike's flight,
the way she moves through wind and speed.

Sometimes she rides toward me,
sometimes she steers far away.

Angels

Do you believe
in angels? The random,
intangible, undeniable seams
which, in flashes & dim light,
mend frayed edge, stitch wonder
from what seemed a bottomless hole.
Divine interruptions ignite bare bulb,
shed sun spears of healing,
of I-never-thought-possible.
Single flutter sets atmosphere in motion-
pattern particles spiraling
toward glistening mystery.

Long Cut

You, housed in your seven year old body
Never walk a straight line
You weave through bushes
Meander embankments bordering sidewalks
Arms out, teeter stone ledges,
Tightrope curbs
Your agile frame veers- zig & zag
aimless, haphazard pursuit of destination.

And I, scurry
hurried & distracted--
admire the way you move through the world
so circuitously
so present
so You.

Easter Bird

The last Peep stared up
from the canary carton
beady eyed & gritty
as if she knew her holiday was over
Evening light danced off
sugar-sheen & glistened.
For a moment, I thought I heard
a chirp, a last cry for mercy.

Then, in a flash of redemption
the Peep took wing,
liberated her gooey body from box
and flew away.

Pie

I notice a billboard slogan,
"Awe is such a small word"
I'm transported existentially.
Brilliant, so true.
It's the small things I tell a student
who wants to drop out
of Life, anxious for 'real stuff' to start.
Real, by way of small:
giggles in the yard, hot coffee,
flavor of pesto & white wine.
One tulip in a vase.

Awe is such a small word, like
sun, kid, pie, yes, and now.

Silly

That is so silly
That puppy is silly
Silly mommy
I'm smitten with this word--
It's fun to say, slides off the tongue.
It's nice.
I want to encourage silly into the adult lexicon.
Silly somewhere fades after preschool—
gets lost after bug loving, the wheels on the bus, and
peanut butter.
It is more than gray putty.
Silly somehow becomes obsolete--
vanishes like the lone sock
into the vacuous hole of dryer.
The middle school-ness of silly warping itself into
"stupid", "retard"
The unfortunate pervasive slinging of high school, "gay"
Finally, the adult morph into "fucked up".
Into where does silly slip?
Would it be a step toward world peace
If terrorists, global warming, gangs and salmonella
became silly?
My worst motherhood tirades –silly.

I'm recommending silly to my neighbors,
to the House and Senate
advocating silly legislation and yard signs.
Bring silly back
Say it
Wear it
Be it,
Again.

No Ordinary Day

It was no ordinary day
Yes, the dishes sat filmy in a sink,
Clothes hung on an outside line.
But the air hummed, made leaves shimmer—
The kind of day that subtly spoke
cinnamon skin of a daughter,
a hundred greens in the backyard.
Thud of mail hit metal box
woke you to walk outside barefoot—
Cement, grainy & cool.
A day you knew you were alive--
Tasted bread of your toast,
undisturbed by neighbor's barking dog.
A day you allowed some slack—
magazines, a nap.

A day when you had to ask what day it was
although you really didn't care--
just knew you continued to breathe
and there was coffee in the house.
A day when you heard the refrigerator buzz
& silence, your dearest friend.
It was no ordinary day
The flyer on you door advertised a block party
You picked fresh basil for a salad, savored its pungent
sting.

There were no alarms or timers
Minutes became hours so you kept reading
You wrote exactly one extraordinary sentence,
closed the curtains and shut off the light.

In Case Things Don't Get Said

In the off chance
We never speak again,
for that is how humans are-
like birds, temporary tessellations
single intersection, separate skies.

In the off chance we fail to voice
the beat of our chests,
squelch lush desire,
silence heart's lyric rap

In the off chance we aren't warriors
never courageous enough to draw our silvery swords
slay our beast
then bury knife & bone
'til spring unfolds in daffodils.

In the off chance we cower & bow
Not brave enough to bear
scars and stiches
that broke us, oozed us open & real.

I'll scrawl this note of Hope--
scatter a few blood-bright words
able to survive a Beauty
we could not.

Poem Rot

This poem sucks.
How does a razor feel on thin veil of wrist skin?
Pick up your own damn mess
Can I throw some fuck-yous in this poem?
The ones I want to say sometimes
but paint on syrupy grin instead.
Can I rant resentments through a poem?
Dislike people that are so difficult to like?

Can this poem puke all my anxieties and regrets--
pin them on a clothesline and leave them there
to hang, to be hung?
Can I tell you to just shut up even though
it's polite to say, "Excuse me, please be quiet."?

Can this poem drink too much wine
and not stain or wither with guilt?
Is "good enough" good enough for a poem?
Can I stay home and neglect every single
responsibility, poetically?
Not take a shower, not feed the dog,
or tell you that really I am not listening
nor do I care?

One two buckle my shoe,
three four shut my door and leave me alone.
Can this damn poem embrace
the throb between my temples?
Absorb pain of a leaky heart?

Who says a poem has to be lovely?
Let it rot on the page.

Somebody Else's Momma

Don't no one talk bad 'bout my momma
'Cause I'm a bust they butt if they gonna
No one disrespects the one who brought me here
And if I need do, with my strap, I'll make that clear
'cause Mom's the only one I got-
she's been with me through a lot.
She the only one in this crazy world that matter.
Anyone mess with her I'd have no choice but to batter.

What? You think you're smart, punk?
You better not be sayin' that junk-
I'll follow you until you're found
And before I know it, comes a deafening sound.
I warned you about my gun
but when I look to see your blood run,
you done ducked and got away
and in your place, a woman lay-
Her grocery bags thrown from her hand,
a child knelt weeping in mournful demand.

Just tryin' to protect what is mine
'cause you know a mom is a one-of-a-kind
so I thought I'd get my revenge on you.
I never thought that her son loved his momma, too.

No Metaphor Day

The poet instructs—
Today, stay away from metaphor.
Don't compare one thing to another,
rather, be with the thing as it is—
white soap on steel sink, cold
water rinsing a glass, sound of knife cutting carrots.
Today, dare be direct--
Do not escape this experience
through distraction of something else
however shiny & lyrical it may sing.

Free of Charge

On a sunny Sunday run,
the rummage-salers box remaining wares, fold card
table legs , jingle tackle box
of loose change & call it a day.

The discards scatter curb sides-
children's mattress, wooden book shelf, a lamp
all wave a "free" sign in hopes of finding a home.

As I squint through the dusky hour,
Maples glowing in autumnal gold,
greens lit up in fire-engine red,
it is as if each spangling leaf wears its own "free" sign-
fall mums & bowing sunflower
sing sublime at no charge
other than my attention.

When You Need To Be Reminded

The first truth
rests on the star-sparkled
value of each inhale, exhale, inhale-
the way you ignite a day.
Single ray beams you from good enough
to worthy, then exalts toward Amazing.

The next truth
carries you in front a mirror where every day
reflects your angels & every day you
shine into the world off that divine dazzle.

Another truth
requires grace – dance your life agile,
tender, ever-opening. Open.

The last truth
is Thank You,
just thanks.

Questions You Might Ask

Does a stone ever feel silky?
How can the wind swirl like strong gray ribbons?
How does Love kneel at your alter
so devoted, so lust-light filled?
Have the geese strayed from migration-
thousands of winged arrows soar into my heart?

When do your hands feel the tiny breath-kisses
sent in sleep, in mid-day after I've held them
for hours to my chest so they memorize love-beat?
Do clouds speak our altitude?
Does a love poem ever grow old?

Or are You&I the gray ribbon that just keeps
whispering through trees,
becoming stronger, silkier?
Have angels and honey bees thrown us
into this random Universe
where we will finally land--- together?

Or have the two bodies we wear always been One?

Greater Things

When it all comes down to it--
if fluff & excess
mattered so much less, so much less
than what keeps the soul lit.

When the bulky burdens, tangled details
Lift …. Disappear….Shatter a bit
and we bring each other back to each other
through the small, the kernel,
to our bread&water bodies-
discard unnecessaries dressed as need.
instead, re-enter by way of beloved breath.
One hand holding one hand.

When we whittle to Joy's core--
those are the moments we
have successfully reduced
each other into greater beings.

Wing

Sometimes it seems there is a wing in everything.
When I wake to disheveled blankets,
thoughts tangle between dream & day-
Time: a thick pain—no air moves, no blood.
Body: suitcase of brittle bones.
Mind: an empty frying pan.
Days I search my flat hands on tabletops,
dig in pockets, page feverishly through notes
completely lost in the bramble of life.

At these junctures, I recall the wing—
one tender vehicle of flight,
each moment, ready to release.

www.ingramcontent.com/pod-product-compliance
Lightning Source LLC
Chambersburg PA
CBHW020520030426
42337CB00011B/481